Very Selected
Michael Laskey

smith|doorstop

Published 2017 by
Smith|Doorstop Books
The Poetry Business
Bank Street Arts
32-40 Bank Street
Sheffield S1 2DS

Copyright © Michael Laskey 2017
All Rights Reserved

ISBN 978-1-910367-86-5

Designed and Typeset by Camilla Lovell Design
Printed by Biddles Books

Acknowledgements:
The poems in this pamphlet are drawn from
Thinking of Happiness (1991, Peterloo Poets)
and from various pamphlets and four Smith|Doorstop books:
The Tightrope Wedding (1999)
Permission to Breathe (2004)
The Man Alone (2008)
and *Weighing the Present* (2014)

Smith|Doorstop Books are a member of Inpress:
www.inpressbooks.co.uk. Distributed by NBN International, Airport Business Centre, 10 Thornbury Road, Plymouth, PL6 7PP

The Poetry Business gratefully acknowledges the support
of Arts Council England.

Contents

5	Between Two Lit Rooms
6	Cucumber
8	Registers
9	Home Movies
12	Driving Home
15	The Day After
16	Picking Raspberries with My Mother
18	The Corpse
20	Permission to Breathe
22	The Clothes-peg
23	The Last Swim
24	Nobody
25	The Page-turner
26	Offering
27	Not That He Wrote Poems
28	Unheard Of
29	Callipygian
30	Ladder
31	A Breath
32	Weighing the Present

For Kay

Between Two Lit Rooms

After work, for once, to walk home,
not to drive, foot hinged to the clutch,
through town, but to walk on your own
out into the open dark,

the Plough, the Pole Star, Orion
distancing you from your day.
Then down the ringing wrought-iron
spiral staircase to the softer

asphalt of the all but empty
car park. One January night.
Such space around you, such plenty:
a good fifteen minutes walking

between two lit rooms, the split halves
of your life, the future, the past.
But for now a skive down this path,
the ridge of the fence furred with frost.

Cucumber

smiles on us too.
From its Latin root
cucumis creeps
through the centuries,
texture and taste
reaching us almost
unchanged, answering
to all but the same name.

Cucumber:
the levity of language
to settle on a word
so mimetic,
cylindrical,
weighty and long,
of a ludicrous
bent like the fruit.

Cucumber:
a licence for staid
middle-aged men
out shopping,
like this one
prodding his son
in the back
with a cucumber gun.

Cucumber
cut for us, bleeds
minute plasma beads;
shows us its useless
rose windows,
its needless number
of seeds. Sixth proof
that God exists:

Cucumber.

Registers

Out of the warm primordial cave
of our conversations, Jack's gone.
No more chit-chat under the blankets
pegged over chairs and nipped in drawers.

Throughout his first five years an ear
always open, at worst ajar,
I catch myself still listening out
for sounds of him in the sensible house

where nothing stirs but the washing machine
which clicks and churns. I'm loosening his arms
clasped round my neck, detaching myself
from his soft protracted kiss goodbye.

Good boy, diminishing down the long
corridors into the huge unknown
assembly hall, each word strange,
even his name on Miss Cracknell's tongue.

Home Movies

By the final frame of the film, before
the tinny rattle of a jerked reel
or that dazzle on the bald sitting-room wall,
Dad had leaped up beside the projector

and flicked the switch, so their shaky story
went ratcheting on, only backwards now:
led in by balloons, bouncing cans and clouds
of exhaust, the car came reversing surely

far too fast at the horseshoe of guests
crowding Gran's gravel, and we had to laugh
at the way our would-be father muffed
his entrance, emerging bottom first

to pose for a moment with his right arm
flung round an untarnished version of Mum.
No sound, just a pan of everyone
cracking up, the storm before the calm

delivery by Dad of some old joke.
Hilarious how they all skedaddled
backwards up the steps into the middle
of the reception, a piece of cake

that a waitress snatched; each hopeful wish
promptly returning unopened to sender
as the knife they were forcing up together
lifted off, leaving the icing unblemished;

a quick balancing trick put the tiers in place;
then unedited longueurs – little movement,
too many self-conscious close-ups of distant
relations and friends they'd lost without trace

and whom we'd never known – nothing comical
except for a slim-line uncle Jim
brightening as glass after glass of his wine
vanished, sucked up by the mouth of the bottle.

It was round about then, while we were all
full of it, paralytic at him
sobering up, that Mum left the room
with a kind of abruptness that niggled

(or would have, if we'd adjusted our focus,
not chosen not to notice) and so she missed
what followed: their ceremonial kiss
outside the church; Dad reaching across

to conceal her face with the antique veil;
and once the blinking guests had withdrawn
into the dark doorway arm in arm
he steered her backwards, helped by two small

bridesmaids tugging her train in towards
the vestry, the moment when he'd unscrew
his pen and one by one they'd undo
their signatures, going over the words

from right to left so they disappeared,
and suddenly the twinkle in Dad's eye
was a hard gleam in the flickering light
and the rare warmth of the atmosphere

too close: not one of us raised the ghost
of a laugh as Dad softly eased the ring
off the finger so gladly held out to him,
or dared interrupt to point out the past

was spilling out, already ankle-deep
on the floor and spreading. He stood so still
we didn't exist. There was nothing real
but that slither of negatives at his feet.

Driving Home

You're on your own driving home,
the miles light music that you spool
from wheel to wheel. Each dip and bend
hums with the tune. It's late at night
and, though you're tired, it's not far now:
the glow shows up across the fields.

A thud, a simultaneous crunch,
and, as you stamp on brakes and wrench
hard at the wheel, a scrape, a thump.
The reeling darkness stalls and drops
a lump of terror in your lap.
The car has shuddered to a stop

facing backwards and across,
so what you see is this: lit up
beside the verge, a buckled bike
and in the ditch beyond, a heap
of tangled clothes. Nothing moves.
A country road. No other lights

in sight but yours. And what you think
at once is this: no witnesses.
You're stunned, appalled. What's to be done?
You can't park where you are. Reverse.
Whatever damage to the wing
it's not caved in. The car still steers.

You know it's dangerous to move
some injuries. You hesitate.
You've never been much good with blood.
Still no-one comes. It might make sense
to drive fast to the nearest house
and use their phone. You must fetch help.

The first place – now you think of it
as you slow down – 's a second home:
it looks shut up, hedge overgrown.
The next's for sale. The third's a farm
down a rough track, two fields back,
a cert for early nights, and dogs.

You check your mirror. Up ahead
no looming lights. No traffic still.
The big house on the corner's black
against the sky. A waste of time.
To pull those distant sleepers back
a bell would have to shrill and shrill.

You had no warning, never saw him.
It makes you wonder. You were driving
well, not wildly; you'd remember
any twitch of fright or tightness
on that bend. You would have braked.
What's likely is he had no lights.

One gleaming window seen too late
– already past and going too fast –
makes you dither, lift your foot,
but then the thought that any light
left shining out along this route
might burn for nothing but that bike

settles it. Why knock and call
through bolted doors, unlock alarm
in narrow halls, explain, explain,
when little more than three miles on,
the other side of this small town,
you'll be beside your phone, at home?

The streets are hollow, brightly lit.
A stray dog cocks a leg and sniffs
along a fence. A couple kiss
persistently. A street-lamp blinks.
A van pulls out ahead, turns right
and, unremarked, you roll straight on.

You kill the engine, douse the lights
and sit a moment in the dark
breathing out. Hot metal ticks.
What's done is done. You know a man
who'll fix the car. Softly you close
the up-and-over garage door.

The Day After

I made a leek and potato soup
the day after, prompted by the look
of the peeled potato going soft
in a glass of water by the sink.
Beyond the back door, drizzle
and the raw morning air argued for soup,
added their weight to the nod of the knife
slicing the leeks, wrapped up in themselves,
into logs, into rings – whites, yellows and greens –
that I agitated till they came clean
in a bowl of cold water and set
simmering with the potato in stock
I'd thickened with flour, sprinkled with dried
herbs – rosemary, thyme – and startled
with a splash of leftover wine.
We had it for lunch, liquidised
with the top of the milk and heated through,
and though I dare say you didn't notice
the taste, you ate it. It's sometimes too soon
to speak about things, but you've got to eat.

Picking Raspberries with My Mother

So little time left to talk
and arrange things that I must ask her
now when we've hardly begun
picking the raspberries whether
she's thought about what to do
afterwards. She's holding out
the family size Nescafé jar
we're sharing and though I take care
I spill one or two as I funnel
the first handful in, cast down
by my clumsiness. She'll just come home,
she says, turning her attention
back to the canes, not keen
to discuss it. This'll be the last
picking – some are shrivelled already
and the rest, mostly small and pippy,
cling on so the trick is not
to squash them pulling them off.
I gauge the resistance, the give
of each berry between my finger
and thumb, and press on. It's a big
operation, I say, bending down
and peering among leaves and the pricklish
stems I push back. Let's not think
about it, she shudders. But picturing
the tubes she'll sprout, the drip feed,
I clear my throat. She won't be up
to cooking and shopping. She'll need
to go somewhere for convalescence,
a week or two till she can cope.

But she won't be pressed, won't look
beyond the sagging cage, her worry
one jar's not enough for the boys.
We've been working different rows
side by side so I know she's picking
some I wouldn't touch, like that one –
dulled purple, bobbles so soft
they're mush on her fingers she's forced
to flick into the pot. Extra
sweet, she smiles. I bite my tongue.

Home in Suffolk next morning a note
from Tim, who came in too late
for supper with the rest of us:
Delicious raspberries x x x

The Corpse

He shares my morning cup of tea, likes it
colder than me. Staring at the empty
blue window, he's my dad propped up
glimpsed again through the ward's swing doors.

I reach for my book, find my place
or jump up quick, wash, give myself
a close shave, inhale soap, and froth
the strong teeth he bares at the mirror.

He's a rude child. I rattle him off downstairs,
stop his mouth with muesli, fresh fruit.
Once I'd kiss him goodbye at the school
gates and get on with my life.

But he grows so fast. No time since
he was nothing but a blink in my eye,
a blank at the end of my tunnel,
yet self-evident now, so conspicuous

in the tube some woman stands up
and offers me her seat. Though my feet
are killing me, I decline, my smile
tightened by his grin. He knows me

inside out. He's like a parent
come to collect me from a party
I've just started to enjoy. Ridiculously
punctual. *Oh, he can wait.* Yes, he can wait.

And he does, exchanging ghastly
benign glances with that corpse
of yours at the way we fret
over deadlines or how badly we've slept.

Permission to Breathe

It wasn't easy. He was still flying
missions then, navigating the Lancaster
accurately into the flak, into the foul-mouthed
shafts of the searchlights. Fifteen shaken minutes
from the aerodrome through the thin November dawn
on his motorbike and he was home. She was up
already with Tim in the scullery
putting the nappies to boil in the bucket.
Only one, the only one, he wouldn't be held,
stiffened against him, struggled and wailed.
It was tiredness, he told himself, tiredness and cold
that had set the tic going again in his eyelid.
Tilted by the child, she poured him stewed tea
and he took it to bed, warming his hands
a little round the thick white china.
Later aware of a murmur in the hall
he guessed she was strapping him in, manoeuvring
the pram, and he drifted off as silence settled.
At the Co-op she collected the butter ration,
at Willis' pig's liver for their tea,
and then she came home the long way round
beside the motionless cloudy canal
where only a mallard made vs on the water.
Tim fell asleep as they reached the gate
and suddenly limp from the broken nights
she flopped down by dad in the blacked-out room.
In that half hour before Tim whimpered
I began, though I was nothing to them.

As they slid apart, one of next door's hens
started clucking and mum almost tasted new laid
eggs for lunch – she'd ask Betty – but dad couldn't take
his eyes off the barrage pounding up
as they came in low for their final drop.

The Clothes-peg

How it had happened they neither of them knew
but it only got worse. He hated the blank
blue ice of his stare and she couldn't bear
her thin voice telling him to turn
down the TV please, to stop diddling
with that clothes-peg, which without thinking he
clipped to the hem of her cardigan hanging
over the newel post as he mooched past.
It was Margaret at work who pointed it out
and all day it kept on taking her hand
by surprise, a bump in her cardigan pocket.
So, naturally, closing his old Noah's Ark
curtains that evening she pegged them together.
A few mornings later it waylaid her
inside her shoe. She snapped it on the end
of his toothbrush handle, so it wouldn't pull through
the holder, and found it next clipping the ear
of Humph, her venerable bear. For him she left it
dangling in the dark from the plastic light pull
in the bathroom, where he lit on the pot
of Paracetamol and dibbled it in.
It felt like a biro caught in his train pass
as he brought it out to show the guard,
and tugging a Kleenex out of the box
she spluttered at the clatter, but said nothing,
just hung it from the lining inside his tie
ready for the morning. And now the drizzle starts
as she's driving to work, she laughs out loud –
lifted by it skimming back and forth
riding on the stalk of the wiper blade.

The Last Swim

September, October ... one thing
you don't know at the time is when
you've had your last swim: the weather
may hold, may keep nudging you in.

Only afterwards, sometimes days on,
it dawns on you that you've done:
just the thought of undressing outdoors,
exposing bare skin, makes you wince.

And that's best, to have gone on swimming
easily to the end: your crawl
full of itself, and the future
no further than your folded towel.

Nobody

If you can't bring yourself to build
a snowman or even to clench
a snowball or two to fling
at the pine tree trunk, at least
find some reason to take you out

of yourself: scrape a patch of grass clear
for the birds maybe; prod at your shrubs
so they shake off the weight, straighten up;
or just stump about leaving prints
of your boots, your breath steaming out.

Promise. Don't let yourself in
for this moment again: the end
of the afternoon, drawing the curtains
on the glare of the garden, a whole
day of snow nobody's trodden.

The Page-turner

He sits in her shadow, keeps still,
as if he would be as invisible
to us as we are to him,
just his eyes imperceptibly moving

till the end of the page approaches,
when, rising from his chair, he reaches
forward, left-handed, and works
a single sheet free, then waits

for the moment to flip it over.
Pressing it flat with his palm
from below so it won't lift up,
already he's pushed himself back

out of consideration. Again and again.
Till the pianist bows, and he stands
apart disclaiming applause,
head down, holding the music.

Offering

When did I last consider my heart,
pay it a little attention, honour
its sixty steadfast years in the dark?
Hardly notice it, my mind focused
on slicing an onion, on what I ought
to have said or done, the story I'm reading
now, Alice Munro, or remembering my dead
aunt Nin's laugh, those half crowns for ice creams.
Yet all the time it's working, beating on
constantly, like a god I forget
the existence of, keeping my blood
moving through its thousands of miles
of tunnels, making it still possible for me
to nod off after supper, to wonder
about Water Aid or no longer
postponing phoning my brother,
to nurse a baby grudge, fatten it up.
It's the size of my fist and weighs no more
than eleven ounces. If I bend back
my wrist, I can see the pulse twitch.
Millions of times. You can do the sums.
That's stamina for you, dedication.
Old squeezebox of mine, what do you mean
by your quiet insistence? What do you want
beyond the few lengths of the pool I swim
most days for you, and my sensible diet?

Not That He Wrote Poems

but in the dream he'd been giving a reading,
launching his latest collection,
and once he was finished, with the audience
drifting off, he wondered out loud
if he'd sold any books. Oh dear friend.
Not only no queue, not a single
hanger-on to shield us from the view
of the stacked table. Precious few
dreams bring him back and yet
what did I go and do, but pretend
not to hear, then making myself wake up,
left him friendless, diminished there.

Unheard Of

Turning back to language with some idea
of the inexhaustible plenty there
restoring you, you're drawn in
on page one by **Abacinate**,
unheard of word, *v* for verb:
To blind by placing hot irons
or metal plates before the eyes,
rare according to the OED.

Callipygian

A thought I have often enough
– it goes without saying – but not
a word I'd ever use
to express it. *Literary*
says the dictionary

but too clever by half for me,
calling attention to itself
when I want language transparent,
not obstructing our simply wonderful
view of such shapely buttocks.

Ladder

Forget climbing up
among apples or,
more conspicuous,
fixing a loose
slate on the roof.
This one goes down
who knows how deep,
a whole other world
that stinks of rot
and rust, and worse,
though most at first,
you'll get used to it.
Why would you think
you'd be exempt?
Lower yourself
into the shaft –
the rungs ought
to take your weight.

A Breath

It was next to nothing, a ripple
of air, a breath of a breeze
through the window, open a little
at the top, that brushed across
my forehead, the briefest touch
as I sat in bed propped up
        drinking tea.

All right, it may not have been
a sudden rushing mighty wind
filling the house, but my skin
sensed it and took in the cool
fluky flow of air that I'm still
feeling the afterglow of
        days later.

Weighing the Present

I didn't believe it for a minute
but turning the corner at the lights
saw him waiting on the opposite pavement
outside A1 Discounts to cross.

Though I didn't believe it for a moment
I knew it was him by the set
of his shoulders and head, that physique
and the all but forgotten lift

of my heart at the sight of him.
For an instant he was alive
or I had died, though I knew
neither could be true and pressed on

to the post office past my friend
with the present that needed weighing,
more or less knowing nothing
was impossible, even heaven.

30 years
of smith|doorstop poets

Moniza Alvi, David Annwn, Simon Armitage, Jane Aspinall, Ann Atkinson, David Attwooll, Anne-Marie Austin, Sally Baker, Mike Barlow, Kate Bass, Paul Batchelor, Suzanne Batty, Zeina Hashem Beck, Chris Beckett, Peter Bennet, Catherine Benson, Gerard Benson, Paul Bentley, Sujata Bhatt, David Borrott, Nina Boyd, Maxwell Boyle, Sue Boyle, Carol Brierly, Susan Bright, Carole Bromley, Sue Butler, Peter Carpenter, James Caruth, Liz Cashdan, Dennis Casling, Julia Casterton, Claire Chapman, Debjani Chatterjee, Linda Chase, Geraldine Clarkson, Stephanie Conn, Stanley Cook, Bob Cooper, Jennifer Copley, Julia Copus, Rosaleen Croghan, Tim Cumming, Paula Cunningham, Simon Currie, Duncan Curry, Ann Dancy, Emma Danes, Peter Daniels, Peter Daniels Luczinski, Joyce Darke, Jonathan Davidson, Kwame Dawes, Owen Davis, Julia Deakin, Nichola Deane, Steve Dearden, Patricia Debney, Mike DiPlacido, Maura Dooley, Tim Dooley, Jane Draycott, Basil du Toit, Christy Ducker, Carol Ann Duffy, Sue Dymoke, Stephen Duncan, Suzannah Evans, Michael Farley, Rebecca Farmer, Nell Farrell, Catherine Fisher, Janet Fisher, Anna Fissler, Andrew Forster, Katherine Frost, Sam Gardiner, Adele Gèras, Sally Goldsmith, Yvonne Green, David Grubb, Harry Guest, Robert Hamberger, David Harmer, Sophie Hannah, John Harvey, Jo Haslam, Geoff Hattersley, Jeanette Hattersley, Selima Hill, John Hilton, Andrea Holland, Holly Hopkins, Sian Hughes, Keith Jafrate, Lesley Jefferies, Chris Jones, Mimi Khalvati, John Killick, Jenny King, Mary King, Stephen Knight, Judith Lal, John Lancaster, Peter Lane, Michael Laskey, Kim Lasky, Brenda Lealman, Tim Liardet, Katherine Lightfoot, Semyon Izrailevich Lipkin, John Lyons, Maitreyabandhu, Paul Matthews, Eleanor Maxted, John McAuliffe, Michael McCarthy, Rachel McCarthy, Patrick McGuinness, Kath McKay, Paul McLoughlin, Hugh McMillan, Ian McMillan, Allison McVety, Julie Mellor, Hilary Menos, Paul Mills, Hubert Moore, Kim Moore, David Morley, Sarah Morris, Blake Morrison, Paul Munden, Daljit Nagra, Dorothy Nimmo, Stephanie Norgate, Christopher North, Carita Nystrom, Sean O'Brien, Padraig O'Morain, Mark Pajak, Nigel Pantling, Alan Payne, Pascale Petit, Stuart Pickford, Ann Pilling, Jim Pollard, Wayne Price, Simon Rae, Irene Rawnsley, Ed Reiss, Neil Roberts, Marlynn Rosario, Padraig Rooney, Jane Routh, Peter Sansom, Tom Sastry, Michael Schmidt, Myra Schneider, Rosie Shepperd, Lemn Sissay, Felicity Skelton, Catherine Smith, Elspeth Smith, Joan Jobe Smith, Cherry Smytb, Martin Stannard, Pauline Stainer, Paul Stephenson, Mandy Sutter, Matthew Sweeney, Diana Syder, David Tait, Pam Thompson, Dennis Travis, Susan Utting, Stephen Waling, Martin Wiley, Tony Williams, Ben Wilkinson, Andrew Wilson, David Wilson, River Wolton, Sue Wood, Anna Woodford, Cliff Yates, Luke Samuel Yates